The Modern Woman's Warrior Creed

Lindsey Wilson

The Modern Woman's Warrior Creed

Lindsey Wilson

Veronica Lane Books

ISBN 979-8-9890770-76

Veronica Lane Books
Books That Make a Difference!

11420 US-1, Suite 124, North Palm Beach, FL 33408 USA
Tel: +1(833) VLBOOKS +1(833-852-6657)
www.veronicalanebooks.com
email: etan@veronicalanebooks.com

Library of Congress Cataloging-In-Publication Data
Lindsey Wilson,
The Modern Woman's Warrior Creed

DEDICATION

I would like to dedicate this book to all the strong, resilient, brave, and worthy domestic violence survivors who have endured unspeakable pain yet continue to battle for their life every day. It takes tremendous courage to leave domestic abuse. The ramifications of leaving can go unrecognized yet your will to survive thrives. I am so proud of you. I want you to know that I admire your strength, understand your pain, and love and care about you and everything you are.

To my closest friends, Michelle Stankos and Nikki Sydnor, I dedicate this to you and thank you for a lifetime of never-ending support and guidance. Without you in my life, I would truly be lost. You are amazing and I love you!

To my "blue butterfly", for your encouraging words and warmth you add to my life with your sweet gentle spirit.

Lastly, to Lori Louck-Campbell (8-6-59 --- 8-15-22), domestic violence survivor, warrior, and my beautiful friend.

INTRODUCTION

Are you searching for meaning and purpose only to realize it was all an illusion? Are you tired of the elemental disappointment of life? It takes a different viewpoint to intertwine life experience and intention, to obtain genuine joy and unearth your unique purpose. We all have been honored with our own path to pursue our reason. Your path will be the only one taken by you. It's yours. It's an intriguing unfolding of events guided by your desires, needs, hopes and dreams. Should you observe a bright, warm light in the distance as you walk this path alone, the moment of finally finding your purpose, something bigger than you, will ignite your soul in a way that elevates your whole being. A level of dominance no one else can touch.

My path was filled with bumps, hurdles, pain, loneliness, and fear. At times, the relief of joy and excitement took over. I struggled to have support in my earliest times. I was missing key elements that coincide with growing up in a healthy and supportive environment. As a result, I've spent decades filtering my emotions and looking for answers to my life. It was a struggle with no guidance or help, and I fumbled my way through it. Medical complications magnified my needs and were overwhelming to take on alone. I used to sit in my room on my bed and attempt to decipher what was normal and what wasn't. It was cloudy for me. I was different and I felt it deeply. The entire experience has been extremely challenging. It wasn't until I became a healthy adult that I wanted to write this book to inspire others and show them how to change their life. The possibility to do it alone, regardless of their childhood or background, is real.

Having the tenacity to continue searching for opportunities to understand yourself and incorporating that knowledge, overall, is what it takes. The answers are out there. There are multiple ways to seek help to figure it out. With the best intentions, professionals tried to help. I discovered no one understood me better than myself. Therefore, I decided to continue my path alone.

The emotional and spiritual growth along the way has changed me in the most beautiful way and I want others to experience this too. It is powerful to realize you can figure out life alone and become your own super-hero. The distinct difference between you and everyone else is driven by knowledge and incomparable solitude that fosters a singular life without outside influence. The day that led me to the bright, warm light on my path, I was alone in the hospital. Staring death in the face, I won and my new life began.

All of this re-birth can be intimidating. The unknown can be scary. However, the greatest lessons are learned through courage. Walking out of it on the other side, you will be a new individual. Learning from all the trials and tribulations is the icing on the cake. So sweet you can taste the freedom. Liberating the constraints of expectations to operate the same as everyone else gives hope and accepting solutions others make for us, vanishes. A different perspective of life will be incorporated into your newfound existence with harmonious functionality and compatibility. A new mindset captures sovereignty and perseveres despite life as we know it. Most importantly, the value of unending peace rests in eternity inside your recharged soul.

Start your new life today and be inspired to believe the impossible is possible!

CONTENTS

GETTING STARTED

There will be many days where you feel like you can't continue any longer. You feel discouraged and ready to give up forever. The task at hand is daunting.

We all face our own battles every day. Some of the hardest are battled alone. The silence is deafening as you contemplate just how much your effort to continue the battle is really worth it.

The battle of the pain, fear, stress, and unrelenting discouragement and sadness that permeates your life every single day. Your whole being: your heart, your mind, your spirit is clouded with doubt. The light within your hopeful soul is dimmed a little more every day.

Whatever your personal battle may be, there is still hope, light, and happiness out there for you. Most importantly, there is still love for you. When you feel ready to surrender to life's daily unrelenting battle to overcome, the core values of the Modern Warrior's Creed will guide you toward the life you deserve—a life of joy, happiness, contentment, and success.

Grab your sword with a hand of strength with a mind of determination and will! Hoist it, high and steady. With a commanding stance, stand up tall with confidence and dominance. Feel the power of the will to win, travel throughout your body. The battle is on! You are capable! You are tough enough and worthy enough to win the battle. You are a warrior!

THE WARRIOR'S CREED!

- ❖ BELIEVE
- ❖ FOCUS
- ❖ DEFEND
- ❖ PLAY
- ❖ FIGHT
- ❖ PROTECT
- ❖ SHARE
- ❖ STRENGTH

- ❖ DETERMINATION
- ❖ SPIRIT
- ❖ INTEGRITY
- ❖ COURAGE
- ❖ LOVE
- ❖ PRIDE
- ❖ INSPIRE
- ❖ CARE

- ❖ ENDURANCE
- ❖ WORTH
- ❖ AWARENESS
- ❖ ADVOCATE
- ❖ CREATE
- ❖ BRAVERY

KNOW THIS!

BELIEVE you can do whatever excites you.

FOCUS on your hopes and dreams.

DEFEND yourself and your self-worth against any force that threatens you.

PLAY laugh and enjoy every day with no regrets.

FIGHT for yourself no matter what and believe you will conquer.

PROTECT your warrior spirit and all you have fought to overcome.

SHARE your winning attitude and grace with everyone, unconditionally.

STRENGTH Stay determined to stand back up every time you are challenged by defeat.

DETERMINATION Use what inspires you to conquer and never give up.

SPIRIT When you are feeling alive and free inside, you have hope that shines upon others.

INTEGRITY Live a life built on trust and honesty. Practice daily habits that strengthen your warrior traits, encouraging others to believe in you, trust you, and value your worthiness.

COURAGE Use your pride and fearless spirit to conquer every obstacle in front of you.

LOVE yourself, the good and bad because you deserve unconditional love and kindness by everyone, always.

PRIDE Stay true to "you" at all times and know your worth.

INSPIRE Use your positive light and spirit and encourage others to unleash their inner warrior and overcome.

CARE enough to change the world. Practice kindness and empathy to all, spreading love and hope to everyone.

ENDURANCE Resist what is easier. Keep going and never give up.

WORTH Take healthy actions every day to create a strong body and a strong mind.

AWARENESS Know that it is ok to ask for help when you feel weak. You are vulnerable but not alone.

ADVOCATE Use your empathy, compassion and kindness to help all others live better

CREATE Express yourself daily and create art that portrays life through your unique imagination and life experiences. Share your creativity and inspire others to feel the freedom of expression

BRAVERY Confront obstacles and challenges with confidence and the will to battle your fears and conquer the world, accepting no other result.

BELIEVE

How can you believe in anything or anyone ever again? Too many people have let you down or treated you poorly. You tried to believe in the goodness of humanity before and others showed you just how right you were to be a skeptic. Perhaps, you proved yourself to be a skeptic of your own thoughts or actions. To believe is to have hope. Without hope, we have nothing.

The worst of life can happen in a split second. Life-changing circumstances will leave you gasping for air as you try to process what was involuntarily handed to you. Adapting to unexpected changes can alter your thinking and motivation to carry on daily life. The ability to continue to BELIEVE eases.

There is an ending for every beginning. It's a choice. A choice worth making. The ending of your distrust and disappointment in others and you ends now! You are beginning anew and that means you change your attitude and believe again. You embrace hope and allow possibilities back into your life. Life constantly changes and we have to adapt as we go. Believe that with change there is positivity and hope and is where you understand that life can be beautiful again. Create a new mind-set and set yourself free.

The creed BELIEVE is imperative because it's one of the most important elements in life. Ten years ago, I was uprooted without warning when I learned I was separating and ending my marriage. I spent over 20 years creating a life for myself and my family. I was in disbelief, looking for a new place to live, literally overnight. Bitterness set in, and I grew too comfortable accepting the world had it out for me. I did not believe in anyone or anything anymore.' To believe was to be naïve' became my daily mantra. Without understanding the circumstances handed to me, there was no reason to believe life could ever be good again. My life was drastically changing. My children's lives were drastically changing. The unknown was a devastating reality for all three of us. After months of turmoil waiting to remove my life and my children's lives from our home and from the chaos, I was given 5 hours to move out of a 3,200 sq. ft home. I hastily packed what I could into a pickup truck, and we left.

I spent the next two years believing that my life was not going to change for the better. The daily struggle to live my life, be there for my children, and carry on was daunting some days. Thrown into a pack of wolves, I felt unprepared for life. I hadn't worked in 12 years. My children are my life and believing they would be ok was always questionable to me. I cared for them for 12 years at home. If there was anything I could believe in that moment, it was that I knew I could care for them daily, alone. That belief is more important than ever, today.

My children were 10 and 11 years old the day we walked away from a life not meant for us. On some days, I felt completely overwhelmed, the depression and anxiety created a reason for me to escape and sleep. Still uncertain about my life and the direction it was going, the unknown, and surviving alone, it all became too overwhelming at times. My mind was left to wander too freely. Sadness was remarkable and I truly began to understand why some choose to leave this earth on their own terms.

On a sunny spring day, my children were away. I was alone sitting at my desk, in the townhouse I now called "home." Unable to recover from my mind fighting to make sense of it all, I sat at my desk in the dining room desperately thinking of something to help me believe in life again. I was tired, angry, and bitter, with no desire to try to be happy or pretend to be. A very quiet house created the perfect moment for the thoughts to sink in a little deeper. My thoughts took me to that old gray grocery bag, wrinkled and worn, and full of old prescription medications I brought along to our new place. Those bottles of random medications in copious amounts were calling my name. I vividly remember the only way to distract myself from thoughts of making things permanent and giving up, was to stand up and physically go do something else. A distraction was more important than ever, and I knew it. As I stood up, the tic tac of my dog's nails rhythmically bouncing off the wood floor, brought me back to the present. Another life-changing distraction and moment to overcome was upon me. I was growing wearier of them by the day, at times by the hour.

I finally got a job, and the motivation to continue started to thrive. I built my support network of friends, co-workers, and family. My attitude started to turn around. I became awakened to the possibility that life could be good again. This continued as I moved away to another state with my children and bought my first home. Who knew I was so capable? Not me. One foot in front of the other, I believed in myself and my capabilities. I believed that others cared and allowed new possibilities for that in my life. I created a new life with hope for myself and my children. I started to believe in humanity again. My life had new meaning, and my confidence to start over and make it, started sinking in. That snowball effect took over in the best way. In due time, I realized when you BELIEVE, you shall receive.

FOCUS

Accomplishing your goals, your hopes, your dreams are always a possibility. The road to get there may not be straight but if you focus your mind, you can control how many turns you encounter along the way.

Staying focused means being mindful. Living in the present is how you reach your destination. To make it, you can't fake it. You live it.

The daily distractions in life are numerous. Some days you will be well on your way to your goals and other days, you'll be parked on the side of the road in a tight curve. Both will be expected. The challenge is having the will to get back on the straight road, with a disciplined mind determined to make it. What's most important is to accept that life will get in the way but it's up to you to persevere. You can restart as many times as you need to, you just have to remain present and be diligent to arrive at your most gratifying and fulfilling destination.

Starting over from scratch is the best way to remain stuck in a curve. I have had to do that too many times, and I found myself restarting my focus and my goals were all going in different directions. Living in the present was not a highlight of my day, to say the least. It takes daily practice to achieve awareness and presence of the mind. It takes discipline to reach dreams.

My focus in life has been challenged in various ways with obstacles and limits. In spite of the rough times in my life, I never stopped trying. To persevere is to conquer.

Whatever is challenging in your life right now, will fight to control your mind and hinder the focus of your dreams. Your determination and will is what creates a straight road that awaits a focused mind.

DEFEND

It takes a level of confidence to feel worthy of defending yourself.

Self-esteem can be obliterated over time. Eventually, embarrassment sets in and the concept of defending yourself vanishes. At the hands of someone else, we have established a new identity based on the treatment of others. The power you have to perceive oneself as worthy, confident, and capable may be buried deep. So deep it's not accessible at the moment. Never forget, it is there! A warrior will instill self-respect and understand that no one else will control a warrior's own self-worth and they will DEFEND themselves to keep it! The words and actions of others do not define you or your life. You do! When you feel attacked or challenged, it is time to start uncovering that fire deep down that is burning confidence and worthiness. The thought that you can stand up to someone else is real. You can feel the penetrating burn to defend yourself. Embrace that and understand you are worthy. Not only are you capable of protecting yourself and your self-worth, but it is also a must! You control what you feel and deserve.

You have the right to defend yourself. Always.

You are a warrior. Pick up your sword and defend your self-respect that is burning on the inside. Confidence abounds and radiates through the sword. Balance your shield and deflect the negativity thrown at you. Conquer all that gets in the way on your path to confidence and positivity. Believe in yourself!

This particular creed has a special meaning to me. Over the last 50 years, it has been a treacherous road for me in many ways. I suffered. To suffer alone is quite literally one of the darkest moments of my life. I have tested waters without anyone by my side, too many times. I have overcome many obstacles others could not overcome. As a result, life experience has created a warrior who is not willing to back down. The longer one is alone, the stronger they become.

I have had to fight alone since the age of 8, which has created the fire inside of me to defend myself at any cost. Jobs, relationships, and friendships have all been a part of my unique challenges as a brain surgery survivor. I have been treated unworthy and disrespectfully by others who choose to be dismissive rather than understand my perspective and explanations as to why my brain is not "typical." I am missing part of my brain. One would think this is enough to suffice that I will do things slightly different (or not at all) than the average person who operates with full capabilities. It is a cruel world. The battle rages on and I have surrendered to the notion that it will be lifelong.

As a result of my circumstances, it has left me with firepower inside that never waivers. Given no other choice in this life, I embrace the fire I feel within and defend myself! When you have had to fight alone, you take on a very singular life and become a mighty and dangerous warrior.

PLAY

We don't laugh because we are happy. We are happy because we laugh. Life is about adventure, laughter, love, and experiences. Life is about embracing playful moments, having fun, and engaging in conversation that shares joy and happiness. We use laughter to get us through tough times. Life is hard enough. Do what it takes to make each day happy and playful. This could be something different every day and that is ok. Feed the soul with goodness. The soul shines bright when the day has been smiled upon!

I think it is fair to say that I embrace life and get the most out of it that I possibly can. I love adventure and discovering new things, going to different locations, talking to people, and exploring local culture or history. Traveling is a free education that I believe we all should embrace. It's an uplifting lifestyle that reinforces the importance of being carefree and not denying the curiosity within. A healthy balance of obligation and fun is ideal and what I practice in my daily life. Getting rid of my television was one of the best ideas I've ever had. Reducing negativity is the fastest way to make the spirit shine!

I surround myself with positive people and light-hearted humor because it makes me feel good. I remove as much negativity as I can and trade it for a life that leads me to thoughts, ideas, and moments that bring peace and create resounding joy.

Happiness is a choice. There is no person, place, or thing that will make you happy. It's your attitude and state of mind that brings happiness. If we view life through a negative lens, our minds will be negative as well.

If only for a moment, understand that life is short and embrace laughter and playful times, with your whole being. Let the little things go. Worry about the big things. The saying, 'You only live once' would be better said, 'You only die once.' Make your life the best it can be. Live it fully and with joy in your soul!

FIGHT

Stand up for what you believe in, even if you are standing alone! Fight to be you. You are unique and there is no one else like you. All that you are, and all that you believe, belongs to you and no one else. You matter. Inflicting judgment and callous assumptions upon others should be deflected immediately. There are so many different reasons in modern society to fight and defend your personal beliefs. Having respect for others is the beginning of embracing change while staying true to yourself. Your fight to be yourself is valid and should be acknowledged. It is inevitable to encounter resistance to your beliefs. Grab your sword and shield and defend yourself and all you believe in. Conquer what challenges you.

Create what you envision your life to be. Finding a cause to support is a great way to express your individuality. It serves a greater purpose and the result of compassion for others is worthy. Your belief system is not to be a judge or be judged.

In your quest to dominate your life and live your unique purpose, understand that others are trying to do the same. A helping hand that understands will always be a bonus in someone's life. Embrace individuality and help others accomplish that too. No two warriors are the same and that is okay.

I embrace my differences from others. When I underwent brain surgery over 30 years ago, it was a fairly new surgery. I was one of the first few people to undergo that type of surgery for seizures. The side effects and the scars that consume half of my skull today are reminders of who I am and why. I understand I am unique now and I use that to my advantage. I'm different. I like that. I live with inner peace now, which took years of curves and bumps in the road to manage. At times, some curves climbed mountains only to leave me at the top, crumbling. As an unwavering warrior, I coasted back down that mountain with confidence and valor and the understanding that those who live in glass houses shall not cast stones.

PROTECT

Finding the courage to protect yourself amid life's hardest times is a valuable and essential part of your journey. Your fight to achieve peace in life shall not be demolished by any words or actions from others. You have found the reason for your perseverance to overcome. Remind yourself that you are stronger, and more capable now, and it is your soul, your spirit, your magic, that deserves the light that still glimmers within.

No one else knows you, like you know yourself. It is important to immediately dissolve any judgments from others or negative thoughts that may linger in your mind. Your mind is the center of your life. What you feed it, it expels. Live a positive life you create for yourself and protect your differences and unique characteristics that define your beautiful soul.

Protecting myself did not come naturally to me. I have lived life in survival mode which often coincides with defense mode. I struggled for years to overcome the external noise from the world that demanded I "suck it up" and "get my life together." There was a lack of confidence as I struggled to make it on my own and defend myself from others' behaviors and threats. I sat on the couch daily wondering if this coercive world was going to take over my life in the same way those devastating seizures once did. A little white flag would gently wave in my mind, as I fought to absorb the insidious words and harsh judgment of others that relentlessly seeped through the cracks of my mind and soul every day.

I spent my entire youth living with a seizure disorder. My childhood consisted of doctor appointments, laboratories for blood tests, pharmacies, and hospitals. I experienced multiple seizures daily and rapidly deteriorated. My life was incomparable to my peers. Out of necessity to cope, I lived in my own world and simply surviving, became my motto.

At 18 yrs. of age, I had brain surgery to correct the life-altering monsters that would strike at the worst of times. The side effects from the surgery now rule my life. With a dose of positivity and acceptance, I have overcome most of the deficits. Living with an invisible injury is one of the toughest battles I fight daily. In the past, the judgment from others permeated my already fragile psyche. Today, as a warrior, I protect myself. I reflect and live confidently that I am capable and unstoppable. The choice I made to overcome was fueled by the desire to not be like others. I am different. I am me. That is good enough!

SHARE

It pays to have a winning attitude. It's also a choice. Good things happen when you share your positivity, winning attitude, and grace with others. Know the limits of self-deprecation and your light will glow as bright as the stars. To believe in yourself is to show others that they, too, can be strong and confident, no matter the circumstances. It's a state of mind. It's a way of viewing life for all it can be instead of what it once was. Recognizing when to say nothing and walking away instead, you will have grace.

We all go through very harsh times in life that can crush the soul. It is devastating but so is succumbing to life's infiltration of pain and suffering. This permeates a negative mind. Instead, be a warrior and rise. Show others how to overcome and conquer life with the right mindset, attitude, and light that shines bright from your soul. If you think you cannot do all of that, you most certainly can! Choose positivity. Embrace the warrior mentality. Be the light.

A lot changed for me in my adult life. I encountered medical problems and became a single mother overnight. I was defeated to say the least. I saw no light, nor did I care to. In survival mode, I chose to just exist. Unknown at the time, rather than absorbing the negativity and bad news, my life was preparing me for something bigger. I am a medical miracle and have survived medical emergencies that most do not. As a result, I came out of the other side with the understanding that my life has a bigger purpose. Upon this new discovery, I also learned just how bright my light shines. I am a beacon of light for many, and that fills my soul with immense joy. Through self-discovery and many years later, I learned why I am here, how to utilize it and give back. As years pass, the realization that my purpose is bigger than me, grows. For once, I can live a life in a world that is not full of pain and negativity and that is aimlessly existing in survival mode. It is gratifying and validating to hear from others how I have made a difference to them or how I helped them overcome. I have been told I am an inspiration for others and to never give up. In ways I cannot put into words, I know this is truly the light of my life and how much joy it brings to my heart and mind. This world of mine is happier, free, bright, and content, and brings a stillness to my soul like a warrior who just claimed victory as they sit in the battle ring absorbing the moment. I deserve that. And so do you!

STRENGTH

It takes strength to make it in this world. To be able to confront and overcome the difficulties, challenges, and unpredictability of our life, is where strength dominates. The challenges we face do not have to be monumental to prove what you are made of. If you have battled with your motivation to get out of bed or fix a meal, and conquered, you demonstrated strength. The little battles matter. The size of the battle does not equate to the amount of strength you have within to persevere and over-come. Strength begins with the understanding that through life experiences and not giving up, you have grown stronger.

Your ability to withstand challenges and your fight to conquer them, builds inside you. We draw on past experiences and what helped us survive, to help guide us. Over time, your strength and confidence grow!

This particular creed is one of a warrior's most important traits. As a warrior, we instinctively use it, and it creates a force within that is indestructible. We stand up every time we get knocked down. In the mindset of a warrior, nothing will stop you from victory! That strength is what expands the confidence you will need to overcome. You are a warrior, a very strong warrior!

Strength is one of the characteristics others use more frequently to describe me. I have spent many significant moments in life getting knocked to the ground, with the option to stand back up or stay there in a puddle of despair. In hindsight, as a child, I was stronger than I realized. I spent more of my childhood deciding whether to be strong and stand back up than I did on my feet, running free.

Today, my life is still a daily challenge that requires a higher level of mental toughness and sacrifice to live beyond mere existence. Part of that is a choice, but my difficult childhood helped me become a resilient and driven warrior. Discovering my purpose was pivotal in my ability to summon my strength more easily and to share it with others. A childhood taken away from me created a brave and valiant warrior where the word defeat does not exist in the mind, nor will it exist in yours!

DETERMINATION

Being determined requires a disciplined mind, a certain mind-set and a tenacious attitude that focuses on reaching a goal. It is your desire to succeed that helps you persevere and attain your biggest goals and wildest dreams. Your level of determination and the outcome of the pursuit is what defines your will. In other words, quitters never win, and winners never quit.

Obstacles in life are inevitable. There will be times when you feel defeated, on the verge of quitting, or contemplating how you'll ever be able to stay motivated to succeed. Part of how we sustain our determination is relying on hope and inspiration. When we feel defeated, it is inspiration that helps us overcome and continue the pursuit. Recognize your limits and take some time to go off course and engage in whatever inspires you. Refuel the soul and then return to your mission. The path to success in life is not a straight road, and neither is the pursuit of reaching our goals and dreams. In your quest to live a better life, it is important to remember that we are all fallible. Be a warrior and fight to do what you know you can do. Once you've mastered this, share it with others. Be the light for someone who needs support or looking for guidance.

Share your strategies and encourage them to keep hope alive. It's never a bad idea to remind yourself and others that if you believe, you will achieve.

One of my biggest strengths is being determined. I think my entire life, even now, has been essential to staying determined. I fight invisible battles every day, yet I do not allow it to deter the vision I have for myself. I have become exceptionally good at tuning out the external noise that tries to knock me down, an essential life skill. A good portion of my life consisted of emotional turmoil. I always tried to stand tall like a warrior, even as defeating words from others penetrated my mind and into my psyche, stained forever. The amount of emotional distress in my life greatly contributed to my involuntary participation in mental games. I have been thrown off the path too many times, and the opportunity to quit has been frequent. My quest for happiness is what keeps me striving to stay determined. I have been working on one goal for over 3 years, and while I am much closer than I was 3 years ago, I still have a way to go. I'm a warrior who doesn't stop until victory is achieved. This mindset will lead me into a life where all I envisioned becomes reality.

Determination to succeed is the will in your heart to focus, stay mindful, think positive, and persevere. There are days when I have wanted to give in to the relentless snags and roadblocks as I pursue my passion of inspiring others to overcome. Perseverance is a quality we must possess if we want to live life with intentional purpose. If I had a penny for every roadblock I have encountered along the way, I would be thousands of dollars richer. It all comes back to a state of mind, the desire to inspire, and the pursuit to achieve. On the days that this is a challenge for me, I make time to immerse myself in my place of relaxation, rejuvenation, and recovery. For me, it is the beach and listening to the waves crash and watching them ripple around my feet. Sometimes only a few minutes in your chosen place of peace is all it takes to refocus, re-energize, and restart. When you have days where it is just too much and the determination is quickly fading, remember getting to the top of a ladder is not one giant leap, but little steps that build with hope, one rung at a time. A disciplined mind will see the gradual climb up the ladder, ready to embrace the lessons learned along the way. In contrast, an audacious mind sees one monumental leap to the top of the ladder, bringing thoughts of doubt, uncertainty, and fear.

The vision of your future and the fight to achieve that vision should consume your mind every day. Feel the fire burning within. If your mind is disciplined, it will not falter on the hope and subsequent motivation and determination to move forward.

You are worthy of all you envision for yourself and your life. It's time to believe, make it happen, and live free!

INSPIRE

What makes you feel inspired to keep going? What makes you feel that warm glow in your soul that fills you with excitement and wants to embrace life for all it could be? You have found inspiration in your life at some point. You are here because you carried hope in your heart and inspiration in your soul. Inspiration could be anything that gives you hope to focus on your life moving in a positive direction. It could be a person, a song, a poem, a piece of art, social media, a quote, etc. It will be different for everyone. Regardless of what inspires you, use that experience to help others understand that life is worth living.

Share your inspiration and make a difference. People feel inspired just by being around you. You have a purpose. Be determined to use your inspiration to influence others never to give up. You have finally found a place in life where you can acknowledge your perseverance and find your calling. I believe our job as humans is to spread the light and share what inspires us to stay motivated.

The pursuit of happiness begins by being inspired to reach for the stars.

Inspiring others is what we are meant to do. To inspire is to find your value and what challenges you have faced with resolve and sharing that hope with the world. Everyone has a story. Share your story. Even if you think it won't make a difference. If you only reach one person, you have changed a life for the better.

Inspiration is a defining element of my life. I strive daily to inspire others and give hope that things are possible regardless of how hard it seems at the time. I find this part of life to be extremely fulfilling. On the best days, someone will approach me and tell me how I have inspired them and why. Validation for what I feel is my purpose in this life, is right at the top of my life goals. Being true to yourself, living your truth, and unapologetically claiming your true self is what others will notice. The vibe is contagious. I am living my life as I am with no ulterior motives, no intentions, no negativity, and I have inspired thousands. Replicate this in your own life. Be you, love and live, and be positive, and you too will inspire the world to overcome!

CARE

Caring begins with a genuine heart that willingly provides consideration, kindness, and compassion to others. It is more important now than ever to be an advocate for caring about others. Society has changed in recent years and has become increasingly more self-centered and less concerned about the goodness of humanity. It is your desire and motivation to do good that will provide you the opportunities to share your love and caring heart. Unfortunately, the desired response may not be what you expected. This is a critical moment to accept that others may not have the same motivation or eagerness to care about others like you. Keep doing it anyway because it is essential to honor your true self. Warriors are loyal to their character and don't submit to societal standards.

I have experienced negative reception from others on occasion. It has always been hard for me to grasp, but I do not falter nor allow it to affect my motivation to continue bringing light to others' lives. To be a warrior and care is to live with the understanding that what you give, you may not receive, which is okay. We all experience life differently, and we must accept this and live our lives based on our own beliefs and lessons learned from experience. The battle to be a light of positivity and continue to provide love and kindness to the world is your calling, your duty.

Caring in spite of what others feel or think can require a certain mindset. A mindset of confidence and acceptance. Most importantly, you cannot take it personally. Any reaction from another says more about them than it does you. Never forget that. Staying mindful and living your truth will assist in this potential disappointment yet heal your soul. Caring with intention and being the "bigger person" is always better than giving back the same bitterness you may have received.

We all need to make this world a better place. It starts with you.

ENDURANCE

The drive you have to make the best life for yourself is exactly what keeps you going during the hard times. Bumps in the road may deter you momentarily, but you endure. Endurance is something we all put into practice every day. In hindsight, we can see our progress but often don't acknowledge the effort we sustained to get us through it. Too often, the focus is on the hardships rather than the successes, no matter how small. Start taking notice of just how much you have endured in life and fought to make it through. I think it's important to self-reflect and consider your daily efforts and how you endured until you overcame the challenge. It helps immensely to maintain a positive attitude. So often, we focus on what we "don't do" or "can't do" rather than what we "can do" and have done. It's a mindset. It requires you to change your thoughts from "I can't" to "I can" or "I will!"

Inner strength and determination are the catalysts to endurance and getting our best life in motion. Even on the days you found to be a disaster, you still endured. Acknowledge that and love yourself for not giving up. Your inner strength is divine. It is ok to accept and find comfort that you are capable and strong enough to do exactly what you set your mind to, regardless of how others make you feel or may say to you.

I don't know which has pushed me harder: endurance or perseverance. I suppose they can go hand-in-hand, but the will it takes to overcome both is an accomplishment for me, especially in terms of coping with a brain injury. Sometimes I lose sight of the fact that I, too, should acknowledge just how much I have survived and the pain I have endured. I believe this is partly due to growing up and living in my own world only to be dismissed, at times, when I tried to express myself. So much of my life is a blur. My endurance, even today, is a result of the will to not let my past influence my future.

There are times when endurance is literally the means of survival. It is during these very difficult moments in life that you should pat yourself on the back and love yourself and believe just how capable you are on your own!

WORTH

There is not a single person who can love you more than you! You must love yourself first to find joy and fulfill the life meant for you.

Knowing your worth is pivotal to living a happy and successful life. The fact is, we all are worthy of the same kind of loving care and special treatment from others. We all deserve the same unconditional love, physical affection, kindness, compassion, respect, equality, and happiness. Some of us had that brutally taken away, but you can reclaim all of it! It begins with self-love. Self-love is to love yourself just as you are embracing your uniqueness, allowing yourself to feel happiness and contentment in the stillness of the mind, and understanding that regardless of life circumstances, it does not define you.

Believing you deserve love and kindness requires you to acknowledge that the insidious, hurtful comments of others from the past, are not your fault. The relentless echo of negativity that you have allowed to resonate throughout your mind, must evolve into positive affirmations. You may have been conditioned for many years to believe just how unworthy you are.

The ability to turn off the tape recorder in your mind that repeats consuming thoughts of self-degradation, hate, and even resentment, takes time and consistency. Change is gradual. Accept that real change does not happen overnight. Replace every negative thought with 3 positive thoughts. With consistent practice, you will begin to realize just how effective this is!

There is a daily exercise that I have found helpful in reminding myself how much power I truly have over my own mind, my own life and my mindset. I call it a "mirror check." When you look in the mirror, don't look away as permeating, negative thoughts instantly creep into your mind. Keep looking at yourself in the mirror as you tell yourself you are worthy, and you deserve good things in life. The affirmations can be modified, depending on the need. This can be done as many times as necessary. The point is, looking at yourself in the eye while positive affirmations swirl throughout your mind, does something. It's called commitment, confidence, and courage, and it changes your perspective. What you found acceptable from others becomes grossly different. You start to create more self-confidence, uncover self-love, and adopt the mindset of a warrior!

Self-love flourishes when you erase the bad and feed the mind with positivity and acceptance. Your value does not equal the opinion of others. We all have certain attributes that we cannot change, as hard as we may try. You must understand that these attributes are what make you unique. There is no one else out there like you. You will fail to grow and be successful until you embrace your differences and nourish them. It is what makes you, you! That is to be celebrated!

Once you know your worth, it does not change. As you evolve, this confidence and power spreads into other areas of your life. It is a glorious moment when comments from others begin to flow as they notice your glow, your positive energy, and your self-awareness of knowing exactly who you are!

Once you have mastered your mind and embraced your worth, you must take hold of your lifestyle. Staying healthy and being physically active will change your life! Modifying your meals to balanced healthy foods is also essential. Practice both together and you will physically transform your body. Be patient as you persevere and view it as a lifestyle change, not a diet. A diet insinuates that it is temporary. A lifestyle is forever. It's a mindset. Once you have the mindset of a warrior, your physical health transforms. Taking care of yourself and maintaining a healthy lifestyle becomes second nature. You adopt the mentality, and the process naturally becomes a part of your life. You'll have others taking notice like never before.

It wasn't until after I divorced that I discovered my worth. It was one of the most important times of my life. The concept of myself was undefined and lost amongst the negativity and influence that had consumed majority of my life. My mindset remained the same for years, and I lived in a world full of obligation and routine. My health was deteriorating, and for

12 years I literally just existed. During this very trying and difficult time, I also raised two children as a single mother.

Undiagnosed health conditions, baffled doctors, and tests of every kind consumed my life. With no clear diagnosis, I continued to exist simply, my quality of life declining quickly. I was held hostage to my own life and my own failing health. My mindset was shattered. Hope was non-existent.

In 2017, my dad passed away. His medical problems just before he passed away gave me perspective and a new outlook on life. In his last hours of life, I stared at his angelic face, reflecting on his life and his struggle to live with a chronic health condition. I decided then and there that I was no longer going to live a toxic, unhealthy lifestyle. My desire flowed with determination to get healthy and live my best life. The urge to finally change my life forever took over.

I started to look forward as the past slowly melted away. My Mindset became the catalyst of my life. The windshield is larger than the rearview mirror for a reason. What lies before you is far more important than anything left behind you.

AWARENESS

Now more than ever in life, we have become reluctantly aware of our faults and weaknesses. Our strengths and enviable qualities are dismissed while exposing our vulnerabilities has become more recognized and celebrated. This shoddy awareness is mostly due to the superior influence of social media, which has created a self-absorbed and judgmental societal monster. A permeating force that supersedes any value we hold of ourselves. It has created hurricane-strength waves of critical comparison. It puts our worth and value on blast as we voluntarily seek validation and acceptance from complete strangers. It's remarkable how much we have given power over our lives and self-worth to cunning outsiders.

Our default to self-deprecation and negative self-talk is presented with perceived criticism, and, at times, even a genuine compliment. We feel doomed at ever feeling whole and good about ourselves. Consequently, a positive mindset is a hard concept to put into practice. The more you engage in social media, the more you accumulate distracting, hurtful, and untruthful opinions about your truth. These insidious projections make it harder to decipher how you really feel about yourself rather than how you are told to feel. What do you do with all of these resounding and presumptuous statements by others that enter your already fragile mind? The relentless question of "Am I good enough?" emanates like a train's whistle rolling through town, bouncing back and forth between the mountains. And yet, as the echo of the whistle fades, your mind stands still.

We have been willfully indoctrinated into life on a cell phone, watching the latest and craziest talent or a silent contest of who has the best looks. This thrusts us into self-evaluation on a daily basis. Your mind may be focused on the activity on the phone, but your subconscious is collecting those emotions evoked by something that really shouldn't even matter to you.

Why? Because reality resides in your own life and in your own home and not on your phone! It's time to rediscover and accept our true selves without outside influences.

Awareness allows us to live in the present and acknowledge all of our weaknesses and relentless internal struggles as individuals. Only once awareness is achieved, can we begin the arduous self-evaluation process without the bias of society.

Being alone in your thoughts and analyzing where you need help is not for the weak. Conceding and accepting are two very different things, believing you are not alone in the process, even more so.

We all have experienced detrimental results from life-altering battles that may prevent us from ever feeling comfortable asking for help. As the saying goes, past behavior is the best predictor of future behavior, and so you resist believing anyone else will ever comprehend your war within. To attempt to seek support once again, you may feel weak, incapable, demoralized, judged, and maybe even ashamed or embarrassed. It's enough to make you want to "check out" for a long time. You are trying to muster the courage to face this battle ahead while silently crying for help. You rethink your attempt to seek help and succumb to the inevitable. In a perpetual cycle, you feel desperately alone and a failure.

Seeking courage to repeatedly meet your own needs is an extremely exhausting experience. Every doubt is the culmination of the apathy once received.

You are a beautiful soul. Your struggles do not define you. Your feelings matter. Your existence is worthy. Exercise positivity and never give up on the yearning for validation and support.

Seeking help will propel you to overcome. You must not allow the ego to win. I challenge you to do just the opposite! Take the risk of reaching out for help and learn that there are times when it works! Identify the biggest obstacle holding you back because you fear failure or more misunderstanding from others. Grip your nerves once made of steel and try one more time! A rare gem with an understanding mind may lie in wait as you proceed with caution.

This creed is the bane of my existence. It is the hardest for me to put into practice. A daily struggle. Though I am a fiercely confident warrior, at times I fluctuate between pride and acceptance. Depending on the circumstances, the outcome could be the difference between winning or suffering. If I do not stay aware of my persistent fight to accept help, I may sacrifice it all. Trying to remain mindful of your needs and when to ask for help, is a duty we must never surrender to. We are stronger when we push ourselves beyond anything we feel we can do or have ever done before. Your best life will come when you decide to go just past your comfort zone. Everything you've ever wanted is on the other side of fear. Requiring help to get you there is going to be necessary.

I often propose a question to anyone contemplating their outcome of any given situation that requires some extra help. "What's the worst thing they could say? No?" Finding the courage to ask for assistance creates assumptions and anxiety in the mind. In other words, if you don't ask, you will never know.

More importantly, you could be passing up a better opportunity or the help you desire!

At times, I feel hesitant to ask for help because I've suffered greatly at the hands of others whom I had perceived as genuine, understanding, or compassionate. The consequences of brain surgery have created a life for me that requires a lot of trust, and I have been badly burned in the past. Removing a total of 5 and one-half inches of my brain will undoubtedly cause side effects and life-long struggles. I have what is referred to as an Acquired Brain Injury. The repercussions present the same as a Traumatic Brain Injury (TBI). It is essentially the same, except my brain injury was acquired by surgery rather than trauma.

Living with an invisible injury is unequivocally the most frustrating part of my life. The number of times I have shared this important information is equal to the number of times it's been forgotten or used against me. It's aggravating and hurtful. Yet I push on. I'm a warrior. Warriors don't allow the opinions or actions of others to dominate their life.

For a long time, I persevered alone, relieved that I didn't have to attempt to explain how my mind functions but wrought with the injustice I had to endure. After 33 years of residual side effects from brain surgery, I have finally come to the realization that it's no longer necessary to try and get others to understand. I have learned to ask for help when I know I need it and when to let it go. I accept that the help may not be delivered wrapped in a bow or served on a silver platter, but I take all I can from their help and use it as a wise and indestructible warrior.

You are courageous. You have what it takes to seek help for any part of life that you may struggle with. This trust in ourselves to believe, perpetuates the good, and the fear of rejection subsides.

The power you encompass to live your best life begins by

identifying your weakest areas and working with someone you trust to help fix them. Believe that. We cannot always do it alone. With awareness, we accept, and with acceptance we allow ourselves to believe. The weakest fake it. The warrior overcomes it!

CREATE

The magic of creativity is real! When we create, we express. And when we express, we are free. Creativity is the nucleus to self-expression. It's where our deepest emotions are attained, and the real meaning of our deepest feelings are captured. We don't have to be "artists" to create. Find a form of art that fills your soul with peace and start creating! The end result is yours. It's your art and no one else's. The beauty of art is that the interpretation is unique to each observer. There's no right or wrong.

It's the process of making art that is cathartic. Your mind moves in soft waves of peace. It takes you to another planet. You disengage in the monotony and stress of everyday life and immerse yourself in your own world. It rejuvenates you and is the perfect outlet when life is barreling out of control. I believe it is helpful to engage in art every day. If you aren't sure of what form of art you like, start out trying one. Choose a medium that moves you. Art comes in many different forms.

You may enjoy painting, drawing, constructing with your hands (crochet, needlepoint, woodwork etc.), writing music, photography and more. If you aren't feeling confident, remember the end result is not indicative of your talent. It's engaging in art and the relaxation of self-expression that makes the difference. And you just might find you're more talented than you ever imagined!

It doesn't require an artistic eye staring at your masterpiece to validate it as art. Be proud of your art piece and share it with others. Encourage others to start creating and feel the liberating self-expression you felt doing it. The focus is not the end result. It's the process. Art is meant to move, and part of being a warrior is helping others view their life in the best light with endless positivity and how to achieve that. There is no better way than suggesting an activity with no rules!

This creed is one of the most important to me. I love photography. It does wonders for my soul and allows me the freedom to be who I am. I have done photography as a hobbyist for over 15 years. With the constant upgrades in cell phone cameras, it's more practical today and far less cumbersome than carrying around a digital full-frame camera and a bag of lenses. The end result may not be exactly the same, but the photos from a phone are getting better every day. My phone allows me the simplicity of doing photography, which I use to make other mediums of art. I also enjoy creating short videos. It allows me to not only create, but to help others. Making informative or inspirational videos is something I would like to do more. I can spend hours doing art. There's no amount of time that substantiates the benefits of creating. Just do it! And remember to inspire others when you have completed your masterpiece.

INTEGRITY

A warrior with integrity will always do the right thing, even when nobody's looking. Temptation is the root of all evil, but the doctrine of righteousness should reside permanently within.

This trait is by far the most important creed. Honor, integrity, and respect are presumed to be at the core of every human. To live a life as transparent as the clear, calm blue waters of the Pacific Isles, the foundation of your life is built. Entrusted in you to always honor and respect this sacred exchange of credence, any betrayal is sure to define a once fruitful life in exchange for an existence of unworthiness and shame. Your success in life depends on a few different things, but good character is right at the top. It isn't worth riding the waves of a sinking ship to be deceitful for your own benefit. Your goal is to make your worthiness and honesty your most prominent traits.

I have found it to be beneficial for everyone, including myself, if I practice good integrity and prove my trustworthiness to everyone daily. To some, even the littlest commitments matter. If you tell your coworker or friend, you will do something for them, be sure to do it! Always stay true to your word. Things happen. Life happens. We can't always follow through on promises or offers when unexpected circumstances arise. However, it's your responsibility to make sure they know you can't follow through and why. Most importantly, you make it up to them once you have the opportunity to do so and as soon as possible.

In my experience, these situations rarely go as well as they should, simply because there is lack of care and dismissive behaviors. The agreement is mostly viewed as no big deal to the person requiring action. Consider that it may not be a big deal to you, but it is something of importance for the person asking. Therefore, it's imperative that you follow through! Respect that and with good character, do it! Always consider others' feelings and needs. Imagine what they may be thinking or feeling. Be responsive to that. With good habits of follow through and listening, you establish trust and reliability with others.

Think of someone you consider having good character, integrity, and value. What are some of their characteristics? Be sure to consider if their intentions are genuine. Implement those into your life as a guide. You can paint a picture of an idyllic human to the most hurt person, and it won't make any difference if this human isn't authentic. You may not have this example in your life to use as a guide. That is ok too. By referencing this book, you can still become a trusting, honest, reliable, responsible, worthy warrior with the highest integrity!

BRAVERY

Bravery is a state of having mental and moral fortitude to confront fear, difficulty, or danger. Mental toughness with a swirl of fear mixed in, is a common nuance of life. How we proceed changes our outcome. Take a moment to contemplate personal acts of bravery or meekness and how the results influenced your life. When we are brave, we defeat.

Confronting our fears with bravery results in growth. No act of bravery is a walk in the park. You feel panicked and freeze. Your heart is racing so hard it is pounding in your chest in perfect rhythm. Your mind is overstimulated and fighting unfavorable thoughts. Decision making skills disappear like a ghost in the night. The conflict of fight or flight is in overdrive. Instinct has a way of taking over and our quick actions reflect our intuition, and you go for it! Afterward, euphoria of conquering fear with bravery floats throughout our body, soothing every frayed nerve along the way. You feel amazing! Pride befalls your weary mind. What a great confidence boost! Acts of bravery prepare us for future conflicts.

Overcoming our fears helps us evolve and grow as we age. Life naturally gravitates toward change. Dare to resist complacency. Embrace your changing life that will launch you into the stratosphere while your peers remain on earth. Meekness will stifle. Bravery will empower!

A creed so meaningful yet so hard to put into practice. It is so much easier to run the other way. Near death experiences are not only life changing but they can also be so random. Arbitrary involvement in life threatening situations can torture and taunt the calmest of souls.

I consider myself a tranquil person. My composure is very good. My calm nature is definitely one of my biggest assets. This soul of mine shines bright in peaceful infamy. However, I had my well-balanced peace tested by bravery when I was stricken with blood clots that nearly killed me.

Alone in my hospital room, I showed bravery that I did not know existed within me. Would these blood clots get loose and kill me? Not one, but two of them waiting to explode. The most difficult aspect of this entire situation was that I had no control over it. The capacity of my mental strength was maxed out well beyond the boundary of my will at the time. Flashbacks of my children filled my shaken mind. Would I ever see them again? Constantly reassuring myself that they must know I love them, right? It's amazing how quickly doubt can take over when your emotions get involved in such a nightmare.

The cold and hard hospital bed kept reminding me that I wasn't home in my own bed where I needed to be. In the

Emergency Room I was diligently reminded by two doctors that I must not move any more than necessary and statistically, I should not even still be alive. They did not want to risk the clots blowing into my heart and lungs. I was frozen like a corpse, literally, in that cold hospital bed but also out of fear. I was too fearful of going to sleep. So, matter of fact, the nurses announced to me that clots tend to blow and people die when they fall asleep.

I fought all night to stay awake. To stay alive. An uphill battle with nature, I eventually succumbed and fell asleep. Oblivious to my bravery settling in, I simply decided to accept that nothing I could do was going to change this situation.

Lying still as my eyes suddenly fluttered open. I quickly realized I had fallen asleep, but I was still alive! In shock, I glanced out of the corner of my eyes at the window and just behind the pulled curtain, I could see the darkest sky. Determined to conquer mother nature once again, I convinced myself I could stay awake till the brightest sun was peeking through the pulled curtains. Perhaps it was meant to be, to give my mind a much-needed break from reality, I fell asleep with the cold covers over my statuesque body. To awaken once again and still be here on earth, is a miracle. As a warrior, my bravery and courage won!

Being a warrior doesn't mean you win every battle. Being a warrior means you have the courage to confront the battle and never give up!

I had to dig deep within my weary body to find the will I needed that night. A calm and disciplined mind saved me! Danger, fear, and difficulty defined my life, and another lesson of bravery made its mark.

CLOSING THOUGHTS

It is my hope that you feel empowered and confident after reading this inspiring book. Yes, there is work to be done but with due diligence, patience, and perseverance you will prevail.

I recommend keeping a daily journal of your innermost thoughts and how they may be affecting this new journey. Keep it positive and encouraging. The goal is to write to learn more about yourself and ways you can change your thought process to become the bravest warrior! It also helps to try to be as specific as possible as you journal. Memories can fade and your reflection may not be what you remember. Having a reference of where you started and how your journey evolves is very empowering.

New journeys are exciting and the anticipation of great things coming is something to cherish. Always think positive, maintain a disciplined mind, and let the little things go. I cannot stress this enough. If you can't change it, let it go! That includes people. You cannot change people. You can only change how you respond to them. Live with the expectation that it is you who you focus on and not others.

Failure and quitting begin with "Can't." Starting now, decide this word will not be used. Replace it with "I can!" and notice what happens! Over time, it will change your attitude which will change your life.

Lastly, change takes time. Please don't give up. When you are at the cusp of wanting to surrender, the life you've been hoping to have, is just on the other side. Keep going. You can do it!

A warrior knows what it takes to overcome and cannot be burdened by an unfocused mind!

Milton Keynes UK
Ingram Content Group UK Ltd.
UKHW050757020124
435290UK00010B/96